CRIMSON STEEL

CRIMSON STEEL

THE SWORD TECHNIQUE OF THE SAMURAI

TOSHISHIRO OBATA

Published by

dragon books

Acknowledgements

Publisher David Chambers
Editor Haruko Chambers
Design & Layout Island Design

U.S. Distributor
Dragon Publishing Corp U.S.A.

Printed by Anchor Brendon Ltd
Tiptree, Essex, United Kingdom
First published August 1987

ISBN No. 0 946062 19 6
L.C.C.C. No 86-73040

CONTENTS

*The publisher gratefully
acknowledges the generous assistance of
Willis M. Hawley Esq.
founder of the Hawley Library & Collection
and Frances Seyssel-Hawley its curator,
in the production of this book.*

———————————— ◇ ————————————

Toshishiro Obata is an accomplished teacher of Aikido as well as a swordsman, and was for many years a full time student of Gozo Shioda, founder of the Yoshinkan School.

Since the age of eighteen I have been a professional martial artist. By that I mean to say that I have either studied or taught full time, and have depended upon my skill in my chosen field to earn a living.

At first I enrolled for the professional instructor's Aikido course at the Yoshinkan Aikido Dojo which was founded and is directed to this day by Gozo Shioda, one of the original students of Morihei Ueshiba the man credited with the development of modern Aikido. The Yoshinkan style of Aikido is very close to the original teachings of Daito Ryu Aikijujutsu*, and its hard fast and practical methods, are much in favour with Japanese police officers, many of whom received instruction at our headquarters.

Since an early introduction to martial arts by my father, I had developed a passion for all manner of these ancient activities, and even the harsh regime at the Yoshinkan did nothing to dampen my enthusiasm. If anything I wanted more, for even though we trained from the early hours in the morning, until long after dark I felt that something was missing, yet as a result of my youth and inexperience, could not quite define it.

Eventually realisation came when I saw a demonstration of real swordmanship by Taizaburo Nakamura of the Toyama Ryu, and knew immediately that this was what I craved. Although the powerful Yoshinkan style of Aikido was close to the methods of the Samurai, and certainly very much more effective than the modern rather weak variety, it was not enough to satisfy me. I resolved to become a swordsman and put my first foot on that path on the day that I left my colleagues at the Yoshinkan Dojo after six years of study under that stern but very remarkable teacher, Gozo Shioda.

I was pleased to find that my years at the Yoshinkan had not been wasted, and that apart from my good physical condition which allowed me to make the most of my training, many of the techniques of Aikido that I had learnt, helped me make rapid progress in swordmanship. This is not altogether so strange, as Aikido is often referred to as swordsmanship without a sword, and both of course were originally armed and unarmed arts respectively of the Samurai.

Having made some progress in the Toyama style (Rikugun Toyama Gakko Batto Jutsu) of swordsmanship, I also studied Ioriken and Yagyu Ryu methods, as well as Nakamura Ryu, in the hope that I would add

*Sokaku Takeda (1860-1943) taught Morihei Ueshiba Daito Ryu Aiki-jujutsu and can therefore be considered as the true link between Samurai Aiki-jujutsu and the modern variety of Aikido.

strength and breadth to my own ability. My mentor, Taizaburo Nakamura is a brilliant, and very experienced swordsman, renowned caligrapher and stern task master; I am eternally grateful to him for what he taught me.

Some time later I was accepted as a member of the Tokyo Wakakoma which is an organisation that trains high level martial artists for work in movies and television. Basically one had to be very well qualified before it was possible to be accepted into the ranks of the Wakakoma, then further, very extensive training was given that allowed the performer to present the true martial arts to the best advantage in front of an audience.

Once trained, we would become armoured Samurai mounted on horseback and engaged in cavalry battles that re-enacted a previous age for the benefit of television viewers, foot soldiers fighting for our lives on some battlefield or even on occasion, Ninja breaking into a feudal Lord's mansion. Our training and historical research ensured that the action was authentic, an important point as we often worked for the prestigious NHK channel, and that injuries were few and far between. It was an exciting and rewarding time in my career that I look back upon with great satisfaction.

So that I could play roles other than a swordsman or Samurai, I trained regularly at the dojo of Motokatsu Inoue the almost legendary master of Okinawan ancient martial arts (Ryukyu Kobudo) and from him I learnt much including the staff (bo), sickle (kama), rice flail (nunchaku) and grinding handle weapon (tonfa). As my appetite for the martial arts remained insatiable, I would also study with Master Yumio Nawa a man with an immense knowedge of the true ancient martial arts such as manrikigusari (the weighted chain) and Edo Machikata Jutte Jutsu (iron truncheon art). He is also the leading authority on Ninjutsu, or as it was originally called in Japan, Shinobi-jutsu, and we not only learnt techniques from him, but constantly referred to him on this subject when we needed authentic information for television shows etc.

While my life so far might seem somewhat eccentric and insecure, I enjoyed it greatly and revelled in the hard training, the acquisition of knowledge and the companionship of my fellow martial artists. Then something happened that became an important milestone in my life, perhaps the turning point of my whole career, although only time will tell of course.

Master Nakamura, my sword teacher, told me that there was a swordsmith called Yasuhiro who made swords that were almost indistinguish-

able from the great swords of the old period of Japanese history, before the battle of Sekigahara in 1600 that is. He had a shop called 'Kanuchi' that was located at Takanawa Sengakugi in Tokyo, close to where the forty seven ronin* of the famous "Chushingura" incident are buried. We resolved to pay this smith a visit and so on my next free day I set off with Mr. Hayashi the director of the Tokyo Wakakoma for the swordsmith's shop.

When we arrived our attention was immediately drawn to three magnificent swords that were on display. One was normal size, about nishaku sanzun gobu, or about 71.2cm, the second a little larger and the third was a magnificent weapon, broad, strong and heavy. It did not require close inspection to see that Yasuhiro put his whole heart and soul into his swords. Unlike the beautiful but rather effete swords that are these days made for collectors, these were strong, sharp, men's weapons that were alive and made to be used. It was easy to see why the Yasuhiro blades had been mistaken for swords made many centuries ago when a man's life depended on his skill and the strength and

* 'Ronin', a Samurai without a master literally a 'wave man', without employment tossed around on the sea of life.

sharpness of his sword. I think we both felt a thrill run through our bones.

I asked as politely as I could if he would allow me to handle the big sword and he agreed, and Mr. Hayashi wanted to look at the mid-sized one. I was very attracted to the big sword, and rather impolitely asked if I could swing the sword in the shop to see how it felt. Although somewhat surprised the smith agreed, so taking hold of the blade by the tang, it having no handle, I swung it. As it cut through the air it gave a whoosh-ing sound that was magnificent, it really was a wonderful sword.

Yasuhiro looked very surprised that I could make so much noise with a sword that was so long and heavy, especially as I was not using a proper handle and the blade did not have a groove. He seemed very pleased in fact, although when I asked him if I could buy the blade he refused because it was already sold. However, he very readily offered to make me one of the same type and made me this proposition.

The swordsmith passionately believed that only swords made in the old way were true swords, because they were not just things of beauty, but made to be used for a purpose. He had returned to the most ancient methods to make his fine blades, but needed a professional tester to test each sword before it was polished and sold as was always done centuries ago. I accepted immediately, I was to receive no pay, but would be given swords for my own use free of charge. My mouth was speaking the words of acceptance and thanks before my mind had even considered the proposition. To Aikido, Sword and martial arts weapons teacher, I now added the profession of Samurai Sword Tester, a most noble, ancient and honourable calling.

Twelve years later I was living and teaching in California when I was introduced to Willis M. Hawley, the founder of the California Japanese Sword Club, and a man who has devoted his life to the preservation of Oriental art. In his extensive library I found many books on swords, armour and all manner of martial matters. His whole collection is absolutely fascinating, and undoubtedly unique.

Among this wealth of material I found a book that gave a great deal of information about a very famous swordsman, Hakudo Nakayama (1869-1958) who is widely considered to be the father of modern kendo (more correctly 'shinai kyogi' or fencing with a bamboo sword) and iaido (sword drawing art). I was surprised to read that far from being a proponent of character improvement through swordsmanship, as modern kendo people think of him, his strongest beliefs were rooted

firmly in practical swordsmanship demonstrated by actual test cutting, an exercise that modern kendo people no longer practice.

I read on and was amazed to find that when he was the fencing instructor of the Emperor's guard during the turbulent years that preceded the last war, Hakudo Nakayama personally tested the swords used by the palace guard on test targets. One example is the case of the thirty swords that were donated by the Shimazu family under the supervision of Vice Admiral Oyamada to the Imperial guard. Master Nakayama tested all thirty but passed only six as fit for use. A few days later, declining the use of the special test cutting sword handle and holding each sword only by the bare tang, he tested fifteen swords donated by the Soma family on the bodies of pigs. Only one passed, and that only narrowly.

When the test was completed, using his own sword he cut clean through the hips of the dead pig to the amazement of everybody present, as this is a very difficult cut even for a master swordsman. Vice Admiral Oyamada asked him who made his sword and on learning that it was made by Minamoto no Yoshichika ordered that the Imperial Guard be equipped with this maker's swords. The very best blades by this smith were assembled, and all were tested by Hakudo Nakayama. Each was used to cut seven times, and of the total number tested, only 490 were chosen for the Imperial guard.

When I read this I realized that, in the first place many kendo people were completely mistaken about the founder of their movement who after all was a true swordsman and that they, not he had strayed from the true path of swordsmanship. I also for the first time, realised why Yasu-hiro wanted his swords tested so badly while he could have sold them for a high price without any difficulty. Both he and Hakudo Nakayama realised that the old way is the only way, and that unless a swordsman can cut correctly, and unless his sword is strong and sharp, his efforts will be futile.

More information on swordsmanship is now available, as is instruction, gradually the tide is turning in favour of the authentic and original in place of the modern and contrived. This is the message that I want to convey in this book. Look back to the old ways and respect them. By studying them you will improve your technique and your overall skill as well as gaining an insight into the way of the Samurai. Much information that has been forgotten is not lost but merely mislaid, seek for it as I have done and your patience and effort will be well rewarded.

In the third century Empress Himiko established Yamataikoku (Japan).

From the 4th to the 6th century documents and contemporary literature record the fact that test cutting with swords was performed on helmets, armour, spears and other swords, presumably to aid the development of improved weaponry.

In the latter part of the 8th century the book "Zokunipponki" was written about the Tempyo era of almost a century before. Records show that test cutting was common during this period as well, and that after helmets and other equipment was tested, they would be used in battle. This constant testing resulted in great efforts by swordsmiths to produce the perfect sword, and by armour makers the invulnerable armour.

In 794 the city of Heian-kyo (modern Kyoto) was established as the Imperial residence, and was known by that name until 1869.

During the 8th century, as warfare became common, the status of the Samurai improved and they became an important element in society, taking much of the power that the Imperial Court and clergy previously enjoyed. Samurai at this time usually fought from horseback using the spear, sword and bow. Sumo wrestling also began during this era.

From 1156-1185 the Heike family ruled almost the whole of Japan and probably their greatest legacy to the Empire was the classic literary work, "Heike Monogatari" the Tales of the Heike Family. From this famous chronicle we learn that Tada Mitsunaka ordered a swordsmith to make two swords for him. One was tested on a bearded criminal and was thereafter called "Higekiri" or beard-cutter. The other was tested on another criminal, and was so well made and sharp, it cut through the body as far as the knee, earning it the title of "Hizamaru" or knee cutting one.

Kublai Khan, grandson of Genghis and ruler of the Tartar empire from 1260-1294 attempted two invasions of Japan, or Jih-pun as it was known to the Chinese (sun source kingdom) in 1274 and 1281.* Chroniclers of the time give different accounts of the events, that of Marco Polo is probably sympathetic to the Monguls as he resided in the court of the Khan from 1275-1292.

The second invasion may have been the invention of 17th century Japanese historians as no record at all can be found in Chinese records of this event, although the first is extremely well documented.

According to this famous explorer, the armada set out but just short of the island of Kyushu a violent north wind started to blow, wrecking many of the Tartar ships and destroying at least half of their crews. Hampered by disagreements between the senior officers who eventually gathered together the fittest ships that remained and set sail for China, the bulk of the army eventually made landfall. Seizing a city on the coast they held if for six months until they were eventually forced to surrender as a result of a strictly imposed seige.

Other accounts, for example by Father Malela in his "Histoire General de la China" paints a picture that is closer to the original Japanese account, and probably more accurate than Marco Polo's who would have received his news of the event from the Tartars themselves. According to this writer, although many of the invasion fleet were shipwrecked, the Japanese were waiting for the Tartars with a large army of Samurai and it was they that soundly defeated the armada. The good Father writes that the Samurai put 30,000 Tartars to the sword, enslaved those Chinese that survived the battle, and sent only three survivors back to the Khan with the news of his defeat.

Although the Samurai were successful in this case against a huge and experienced army, they learned two lessons that would change the way that battles in future would be fought. The first was that the custom of the senior Samurai addressing the enemy with details of his name heritage etc. died out as a result of the Tartars surrounding them with a mass of foot-soldiers while they performed this pre-battle ritual which was an essential part of Samurai etiquette, and cutting them down. The second was the need to make the Samurai swords, sharper and lighter in order to cut more easily through the tough leather armour worn by the Tartars.

During the Kamakura era there were reputedly, many famous swords made. The swords of Kanenaga and Sanjo Munechika were said to be able to cut through large stones, and massive tree trunks. This is obviously an exaggeration of their cutting power however, many magificent swords were made during this period and there obviously was a great deal of test cutting being done.

In 1333 the Kamakura Government was overthrown later to be replaced in 1338 by the Muromachi Bakufu under Ashikaga Takauji who became Seii Tai Shogun.*His descendant the third Shogun Yoshimitsu,

---

*originally a title applied to Generals sent to quell disturbances in Eastern Japan it was adopted by Tokugawa Ieyasu as a description of his rank, and he was afterwards described as Shogun meaning supreme military commander.

ordered the sixty best swordmakers in the Japanese empire to produce swords from which he would choose those that would be elevated to the status of 'treasure'. As swords at that time were valued primarily for their sharpness, all were used for test cutting before the best were chosen. Batto-jutsu, the simultaneous drawing and cutting technique using a sword worn edge upwards, was developed during this period, reputedly by Hayashizaki Shigenobu.

The death of the 6th Shogun Ashikaga Yoshinori in 1441 at the hands of Akamatsu Mitsusuke, ushered in the Sengoku Era, a time of almost continuous warfare that resulted from the sudden decrease in the authority of the Shogun, and the political vacuum that this created. Samurai were kept on a constant state of alert, as province would attack neighbouring province without warning in the hope of extending their territory. The testing of swords became an essential activity for the professional fighting man who at any time would be required to go into action, and needed to have complete confidence in his weapons.

One regrettable consequence of the need for weapon testing was the custom of 'Tsuji-giri' the cutting of live human beings, either criminals, or even in some cases innocent passers by. Although illegal, and very much against the Samurai's ethical code, this practice was common for a while during the Sengoku era and just prior to the Edo period. Toyotomi Hidetsugu, the younger brother of Taiko* Toyotomi Hideyoshi was notorious in this respect performing test cutting on live criminals, innocent victims and even his own retainers. This behaviour earned him the name of "Sesho Kampaku" or murderous Lord.

It was during the Sengoku era that test cutting became formalised. First, Anyoji Kaga No Kami devised a formal method for cutting, but this practice seems to have died with him. At around the same time, but independently, a tradition was started by Tani Dewa No Kami that was to prove more enduring. This famous swordsman at first served Saito Dosan, then later Oda Nobunaga and finally Toyotomi Hideyoshi. Distinguishing himself at the battle of Honganji in 1576 by killing five famous Samurai from the opposing army, he earned for himself a citation for bravery from Oda Nobunaga. Three years later at the battle of Miki castle Tani Dewa No Kami was killed at the age of fifty. During his lifetime he laid down the basis for formalised test cutting that would become in the course of time the Tani School.

*Toyotomi Hideyoshi, being of relatively humble birth could not take the title of 'Shogun' despite the fact that he ruled the whole of Japan and had to be satisfied with the position of Kanpaku. When he retired he took the title of 'Taiko'.

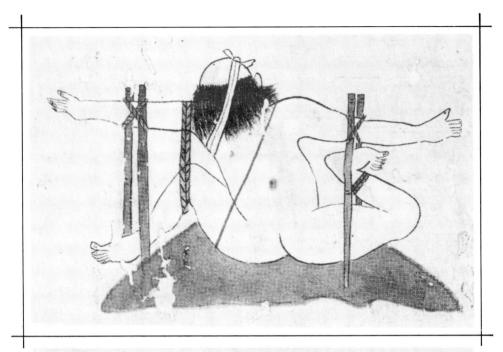

Bodies fixed in position ready for test cutting. The path the sword should follow is shown in both cases by a dark line.

Immediately after his death, his third son saved his family from disgrace and at the same time secured a fine reputation for himself, by attacking and killing his father's killer, and recovering the body of his parent. Tani Yasutomo was for his bravery awarded a citation by Toyotomi Hideyoshi. Although his father actually invented the formal method or "kata" for test cutting, his third son is credited with opening the first school to teach the Tani Ryu method, and was known to have practised his method on dead bodies throughout his lifetime. A great hero in his own right, he was honoured by the gift of a Kunimitsu sword of great value from Hideyoshi who also bequethed to him a famous short sword known as the "Tsurigiri".

Shortly thereafter he became a professional sword tester and went on to serve Tokugawa Ieyasu with great distinction both at Sekigahara in 1600 and the winter and summer campaigns at Osaka castle fourteen years later. He was greatly honoured by Tokugawa Ieyasu, allowed an income of 16,000 koku* of rice, (a princely sum by the standards of the time) and granted Tamba no Kuni (Kyoto area) as his fief. He died in 1627 on December 23rd at the age of 65.

The Tokugawa period heralded a time of peace and relative prosperity. The warfare between rival provinces was not permitted, hostages from all provincial aristocratic families were kept as 'guests' in the capital city of Edo, and the political balance therefore, rigidly maintained. The Samurai with little to do, other than attend to purely ceremonial duties and settle the occasional dispute, were not the men of two centuries earlier. However, in some areas the old ways were very carefully preserved. The foundations laid by Tani Dewa No Kami and his illustrious heirs would not be wasted, although the direction that they would take would be a somewhat different one.

*a koku of rice equals approximately four and one half bushels.

The Peaceful Years

During the rule of the Tokugawa Shogun, the Samurai were given few opportunities to test their mettle or their skill at swordsmanship other than in disputes of honour. It is true that the Shimazu Clan subjugated the Islanders of Okinawa in 1609, although this did not amount to a victory of great consequence or special value, as the islanders were mainly peasants, and although they fought courageously, were no match for the Samurai from Kyushu.

One of the few chances for employment arose in 1637 when the Shogun raised an army to put down a revolt by Japanese converts to Christianity. The Shimabara incident was not a deed that was steeped in honour, or particularly glorious. The thirty seven thousand Christians were besieged in the Castle of Shimabara with the forces of the Shogun ranged about them. Several incidents, other than the eventual fall of the castle and the death of all but one of its defenders, make the incident interesting however.

Firstly it seems to be the last event of its type at which espionage agents or Ninja were used. As it was, the Ninja from Iga prefecture performed very poorly and only managed to steal some rice from inside the castle. Attempting another break-in, several fell from a wall injuring the reputation of the Iga Ninja as much as themselves, and effectively ending a one thousand year tradition of espionage and organised mayhem.

Secondly, it was one of the last battles that Miyamoto Musashi took part in, and one of the few in which he was injured. Although he would by the time of his death have emerged victorious from more than sixty duels killing considerably more than sixty men in the process, at Shimabara he was injured by a stone thrown from the battlements by a woman. His stepson noted at the time that Musashi bemoaned the loss of some of his youthful vigour, claiming that in his earlier days he would have been able to avoid such an injury without difficulty.

The final result of this campaign, was the extermination of the Catholic faith in Japan and the issuance of a monumental degree. After years of interference in their domestic affairs by Jesuit and Franciscan 'missionaries', the Japanese acted.

Blaming the whole Shimabara incident on the Portugese the Shogun issued this proclamation:–

> **"**No Japanese ship or boat whatever, nor any native of Japan, shall presume to go out of the country: who so acts contrary to this shall die, and the ship with the crew and all goods aboard shall be sequestered till further order.
>
> All Japanese who return from abroad shall be put to death. Whoever discovers a priest shall have a reward of 400 to 500 shuets* of silver, and for every christian in proportion.
>
> All persons who propogate the doctrine of the Catholics, or bear this scandalous name, shall be imprisoned in the common jail of the town.
>
> The whole race of Portugese, with their mothers, nurses and whatever belongs to them shall be banished to Macao.
>
> Whoever presumes to bring a letter from abroad, or return after he has been banished, shall die with all his family; also whoever presumes to intercede for him shall be put to death. No nobleman or any Samurai shall be suffered to purchase anything from a foreigner.**"**

Every Catholic was now made to pay the price for the disgraceful behaviour of Spanish and Portugese priests over the years, priests that were originally sent to Japan not so much to claim the country for God and the holy catholic church, but to create a trade monopoly for their respective countries as well as the Pope in Rome, and grow fat on the proceeds.

As peace once again reigned, demoralisation of the Samurai was widespread until in 1701 an incident occurred that to some extent rekindled the Samurai spirit among that class of society, and even raised the status of the professional fighting man in the eyes of the populace in general. The case of the forty seven ronin became so famous that its subsequently has been one of the most common and best loved subjects of theatrical productions and wood block art.

The incident happened in the Shogun's palace between two noblemen, one of exalted rank. After being repeatedly insulted by Kira Kozuke no Suke the Master of Ceremonies, Asano Takumi No Kami drew his short sword within the confines of the palace and injured him. He was immediately sentenced to Seppuku or Hara Kiri as it is commonly called, and died shortly afterwards at his own hand.

---

*approximately five ounzes of silver equals one shuet.

Asano Takumi no Kami Lord of Ako, his action in defending his honour gave rise to the forty seven ronin incident.

After his death, the ranks of his retainers dwindled until only 47 led by Oishi Kura no Suke remained and they, as had been the way of Samurai since time immemorial, swore to avenge their Lord. They also intended that their action would be a joint protest at the injustice of the sentence that condemned their master to death, as Samurai law decreed that as both principals were at fault, both should be punished equally. For months they were followed everywhere by Lord Kira's spies, ever alert to the possibility that the masterless Samurai or "Ronin" as they were known would attempt revenge. Eventually by leading dissolute lives of drunkeness and debauchery, and in some cases even abandoning their wives and families, Lord Kira was persuaded that the danger of his own death at the hands of this drunken rabble no longer existed and he called off his spies.

Kira Kozuke no Suke, Grand Master of Ceremonies, although equally at fault for insulting Lord Asano he was not punished.

On December 14th 1702, the loyal retainers collected the weapons that had long been hidden, met as they had planned many months before and on a crisp winter night, the ground covered by a thick carpet of the purest white snow, proceeded to the Kira mansion. Having advised the neighbours that they were about to settle a matter of honour and not commit a crime, they furiously attacked the Kira mansion and after fierce fighting overcame all resistance. Lord Kira was given the opportunity to kill himself honourably as was the custom but was unable to do so. At this point one of the Ronin took his head and carrying it to the final resting place of their Lord, placed it upon his grave.

When the forty seven Samurai overcame the guard on the Kira Mansion, they eventually found their enemy hiding in the fuel shed.

不和勝左ヱ門

竹林定七

髙野師直

一蕙齋芳艶

As Lord Kira was during his lifetime an influential man of considerable wealth and rank, all forty seven Ronin were eventually, and after much indecision by the government which was split equally between those who wanted to free them and those that thought they should die, sentenced to self-extermination. The sentence was carried out on February 4th 1703, much to the displeasure of the general public. They, as tradition dictated, felt that no man should be forced to live under heaven with the murderer of his Lord, and great sympathy and respect was generated for the stalwart Samurai and their noble cause. This incident persists in the minds of the Japanese as the perfect example of the high moral and spiritual values of the true Samurai. *As can be seen from the above, from the time that Osaka Castle fell in 1615 until the Meiji restoration in the second half of the 19th century that signalled the end of the Tokugawa line of Shoguns, there was little practical outlet for swordsmen, with the exception of one particular elite group that worked directly for the government. The occupations of sword tester and executioner were separate but sometimes performed by the same person. In fact, one family dominated both positions for eight genera-tions, and carried on the work that was started by Tani Dewa no Kami almost from the time of his death until execution by decapitation was abolished in the 15th year of the Meiji period. [1882].

---

* It is widely believed that actually 48 retainers took part in this act of revenge, forty seven Samurai and one servant, a foot soldier (ashigaru). It was he who carried the news of their action to their respective families together with their last messages and keep-sakes. After the death of his colleagues, he became the caretaker of the cemetery in which they were buried with their Lord.

As the Tokugawa government was essentially a military one, and the Shogun actually a generalissimo rather than a civilian head of state, the government was run on military lines. This extended to the appointment of an official sword tester to the Shogun, selected from the finest swordsmen in the land, and exhalted to a high social standing upon his appointment to this position.

Following the death of Tani Dewa no Kami, this position was taken by his best student Nakagawa Saheita who apart from his expertise with the sword, was also a noted master of Yoshida style archery and instructor to the third Tokugawa Shogun Iemitsu. An educated man, his skill at sword testing was obviously highly valued as swords still exist that are marked with his name.

His premier student was a man called Yamano Kaemon, a self taught swordsman who, dissappointed with his lack of progress his solitary study brought him, became a student of the Shogun's sword tester. His improvement thereafter was rapid. Every morning he would perform 3,000 practice swings followed by a further 800 at sunset. Although as his skill increased he was asked to test many swords, he greatly favoured those of the famous smith Kotetsu, and in fact the combination of Yamano's technique and Kotetsu's* blades aided the reputation of both greatly.

The recommendation of his teacher Nakagawa Saheita got him the job of official sword tester, and he also took the job of the executioner to further his technique. During the next 30 years, he beheaded 6,000 convicted criminals, as many as 27 in one day. He retired at the age of forty eight years old, but was recalled from time to time by the government to test swords. The absolute professional, he would listen to the cutting technique of other swordsmen and could tell by the sound alone whether the cut was a good one, and the neck therefore, cut cleanly through.

Yamano Kanjuro, son and successor to Yamano Kaemon, seems to have had a robust sense of humour as this story illustrates. One day he noticed a man going about his business carrying a large water melon on his shoulder. Following him without being noticed, he drew his sword "nuki uchi" fashion and cut cleanly through the melon without touching the shoulder of the man carrying it. He, seeing a swordsman unsheath his blade and cut at him, and observing the apparently bloody remains

*Kotetsu is for many, the premier swordsmith of the Edo period, and his blades are highly rated. Originally an armour maker, at the age of fifty he went to Edo and set up as a swordsmith.

Warfare in the early periods of Japanese history took the form of a large number of individual battles between Samurai of two factions, rather than a conventional battle between opposing armies.

roll along the street, took it to be his head and chased after it much to the amusement of the local people.

Kanjuro had two notable students, Ugai Jurozaemon and Yamada Asaemon who were classmates. Ugai Jurozaemon was fortunate in being appointed the official sword tester to the 4th Tokugawa Shogun in 1692, and during his career tested many famous swords including blades by Masamune, Kunitoshi, Rai Kunimitsu, Aoe Masatsune, Nagamitsu, Sukenaga and others. As a special honour he was allowed to display his family coat of arms on the gate of his house (Teimon) a privilege only normally allowed to feudal Lords (Daimyo) and the Tokugawa family's personal physician.

As were his predecessors, he seems to have been a good and compassionate man, who possessed a sense of humour. One evening during the performance of a tea ceremony at the Matsudaira Mansion, an unpardonable mistake was made by one of the guests who was promptly ordered to be put to death. Jurozaemon, asked, then insisted that he take the person and carry out the sentence, to which the others present agreed. Taking the unfortunate to his home, he tied him beneath the body of a dead criminal then taking his sword in both hands, gave a mighty shout bringing the sword down and through the body of the criminal, but stopping short at the victim of circumstance who lay beneath.

Amid peels of laughter, Jurozaemon told his would-be victim that even a professional executioner occasionally made a mistake and therefore he was free to go. This warmth of feeling for his fellow beings seems to have been the reason why he ceased officiating at executions on March 2nd 1700 after performing 1,505 decapitations. He passed away in 1710.

From this time forward, eight generations of the Yamada family all bearing the given name of Asaemon, filled the office of sword tester to the Tokugawa Shogun, a position in which they earned the nick name of "Kubikiri Asaemon" or Asaemon the Neck Cutter".* Their tenure did not cease until 1882 when this form of capital punishment was abolished. By performing their duty, the practical technique of swordsmanship was kept alive despite almost three centuries of peace.

*It is interesting to note that even today being dismissed from one's employment is referred to in everyday Japanese as having one's neck cut.

In 1867 the Meiji Restoration returned supreme power to the Emperor after almost a thousand years of military rule. Then in 1876 the Rikugun Toyama Gakko a military academy for the training of the new western style army was opened and included in its curriculum swordsmanship and bayonet practice. A unique, and totally practical style of swordsmanship was developed at the academy based on the expertise of the greatest living swordsman of the period, and became known as Toyama Ryu. An essential part of the training was the use of realistic practice targets to test the cutting ability, and thereby the technique of the student swordsman. Therefore, while many schools of swordsmanship became public property and as a result lost their vitality, the techniques of feudal Japan's professional fighting man, were passed directly to the new Samurai by virtue of the establishment of the Toyama Academy. Three years after the establishment of the Toyama School, the 'Haito Rei' law was enacted and the wearing of swords forbidden; from that time forth only the military and the police would be allowed arms.

From the 3rd until the 8th century A.D. swordsmanship was referred to as 'Tachi Uchi' or 'Tachi Kaki'. In later eras it was known as 'Heiho', 'Toho' or 'Kenpo'. Later still it would be called 'Gekiken', 'Kenjutsu' and finally 'Kendo'. This should not be confused with the modern derivative sport of kendo, which is more correctly referred to as 'shinai kyogi' the name that it was given around 1950. "Shinai kyogi" is not of course true swordsmanship, but a modern sport loosely based upon the principles of swordsmanship.

In ancient times prior to the Gempei Era [1156-1185] technique lacked refinement and consisted mainly of striking with as much power as possible at the enemy in order to defeat him. Battles in this period were generally commenced with mounted cavalry and archers, then as the distance closed, spears halberds and swords would be employed, both from horseback and by infantry. Swords were worn slung from hangers, edge down, and had to be removed from the scabbard before being used.

During the turbulent years of the Sengoku Era that followed, continuous organised warfare diminished and sneak attacks became more common. The end result was the development of the Katana, a sword of less curvature than the tachi and therefore easier to draw, that was worn edge upwards through the Samurai's sash. In this position with the handle directly in front of the stomach, the grip could be quickly grasped, and by twisting the scabbard to the side, the blade 'jumped' forward in a raking, slashing motion that if skillfully performed could injure an enemy before he could draw his own weapon, or at least restore the balance in a fight against a swordsman with sword already drawn. Batto-jutsu, the simultaneous draw and cut became an important skill that all Samurai worked hard to acquire. Even the aristocracy felt it necessary to acquire some expertise in this area during these dangerous times.

The basic cutting techniques seem to have been formalised at this time as can be seen from entries in the Sendai Date family's chronicle, still in existence which refers to 'ogamigiri' a forward vertical cut (Toyama Ryu terminology shinchoku-giri) 'narabegiri' a sideways horizontal cut (mayokogiri) and 'gyakuagegiri also called 'gyakukesa' the name still used by Toyama swordsmen. At the same time 'Kenkyaku' or master swordsmen appeared, and with them formal schools of swordsmanship that were clan based or limited to one geographical area. Three of the oldest schools are Tenshinseiden Katori Shindo Ryu, Kage Ryu and Nen Ryu.

The founder of what was first called 'Kage Ryu', Kamiizumi Ise no Kami, was born in 1508 and was by all accounts a most proficient swordsman. At the age of thirty five he changed the name of his method to Shinkage Ryu. He is also remembered for his development of the 'fukuro shinai' the split bamboo sword covered in leather that is still used by swordsmen of this school today.

The founder passed his knowledge onto Yagyu Sekishusai who in turn taught his fifth son Yagyu Tajima No Kami Munenori, who is responsible for changing the name of the school to Yagyu Shinkage Ryu. This prolific swordsman would in the fullness of time instruct Tokugawa Ieyasu, the second Tokugawa Shogun, Tokugawa Hidetada and the third Shogun, Iemitsu. In return for his services he received the handsome stipend of 10,000 Koku of rice and was promoted to the rank of 'So Metsuke'. A close friend of the renowned Zen monk Takuan Zenji, he was until his death at the age of 76 a special adviser to the Shogun. Until the Meiji Restoration, the Yagyu family provided instructors to the Tokugawa family.

Nen Ryu was a style that had its roots in the Muromachi era when it was the favoured school of the Ashikaga Shoguns. Its influence spread over a large area, and from it many other, related styles grew, the best known being Itto Ryu. At the beginning of the Edo period, Miyamoto Musashi founded Niten Ichi Ryu. A scholarly warrior, or vicious ruffian depending on whose version of history you believe, he certainly was a most successful swordsman beating more than sixty opponents during his career.

His style was distinguished by the use of two swords, not so much in combat but in training, so that the swordsman would learn to be ambidextrous, and therefore capable of not only defending himself but actually attacking, even when wounded in his sword arm. Realising the importance of this principle, Toyama Ryu also trains its students in the use of the sword in either hand. Contrary to popular belief, and the impression given by the many woodblock prints that were made of him long after his death, he almost invariably used a single sword held with both hands in the duels that he fought.

At the beginning of the Edo period there were around two hundred schools of swordsmanship in existence most of which, with the exception of those that were adopted by the military and became part of Toyama Ryu, have become the casualties of time. Many so called 'old schools' claim to teach the original methods of their founders, but almost without exception they have lost their vigour, as a result of

By the 16th century many styles of swordsmanship had evolved. This plate from the book Heiho Okugi Sho, (the inner secrets of martial strategy) written by the Takeda clan strategist Kansuke Yamamoto around 1580, shows stances and movements, while the accompanying text gives practical hints on application.

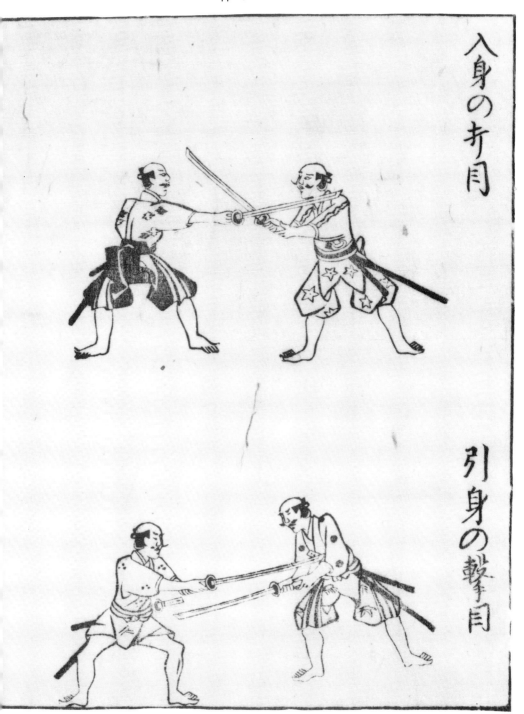

入身の打月

引身の撃月

their techniques remaining untested during the peaceful years of the Tokugawa period. Their claims to authenticity must therefore be viewed with a fair amount of scepticism, and certainly the methods that they teach are in many cases impractical and in others, quite bizarre.

In 1876 the wearing of swords was outlawed, and the rank of Samurai slipped into history. Swordsmanship was regarded as a useless relic of the past and all but died out, its introduction into the syllabus of the Toyama Ryu was one of the two factors that saved it from complete destruction. The other was the determination of traditionally minded families in outlying districts to maintain the customs they valued so highly.

The new military was drilled by French and German instructors, equipped with European style uniforms and trained to fight as a modern army. Even the traditional sword, for drill and ceremonial wear at least, was replaced by the European style sabre for a time. However, as a result of experiences in the wars against China and Russia in which the new Japanese Army barely thirty years after its formation, achieved conclusive victories, the military changed back to the Samurai sword because of its much greater effectiveness in actual combat conditions.

The new confidence of the Japanese people, and growing nationalism produced a renewed interest in the martial arts and they once again became popular. However, these were not so much the powerful fighting methods of the Samurai designed to at least fatally wound an opponent or preferably kill him outright with one blow, but new 'modified' methods aimed at 'spiritual improvement' and 'character polishing'. Fundamental principles of the Samurai were ignored as the new forms of swordsmanship were further diluted.

For example, the Samurai never wore his long sword when seated because it was not worn into the house, yet "Iaido" as the new sword drawing art was termed, taught many sword drawing methods from the formal seated "seiza" position. Additionally, the forward cut on unsheathing the sword became a dismal slice, and the cleaning and resheathing of the sword more a theatrical display than the conclusion of a fatal struggle. Spirit polishing rapidly degenerated into ego polishing, and much of what the Samurai treasured in their arts disappeared for ever from the modern 'budo' disciplines.

During the last war, graduates of the Toyama School went into battle with swords their Samurai ancestors would have felt comfortable with, and served with distinction. American military journals are peppered with references to Toyama swordsmen who caused serious damage

By the time the war against China started, the Japanese army was almost indistinguishable from a European one of the period.

both physical and psychological when they emerged from trenches at the head of their troops, sword held high and a scream on their lips. In China the Nanpo Kirikomitai (Special Southern Attack Force) went into action armed only with swords, and created havoc whenever they engaged the enemy. The spirit of the Samurai was alive in the Toyama Ryu and even after the hostilities ended with the defeat of Japan, was kept alive by a few swordsmen that had served in its ranks.

Recently authentic swordsmanship has been enjoying a revival and the number of students has increased greatly. Instruction is becoming more readily available around the world, and the printed word is also helping the spread of knowledge. It can only be hoped that through this growth in interest, the sword techniques of the Samurai will continue to be studied, and that through them we will understand more about Japan, its history and people.

6

Ichimonji Suburi

一文字素振り

Ichimonji or single line practice cutting is an important exercise for students of all levels of ability, and should be practised frequently. At beginner level it is recommended that the student cut all the way down to the lower of 'gedan' level on every swing, while more advanced students can vary their exercise to include cuts to 'jodan' upper and 'chudan' middle levels. This exercise will develop good co-ordination between the swordsman and his weapon, and should therefore be practised on both left and right hand sides to ensure balanced development of technique.

1. From the 'attention' position . . .

2 . . . draw your sword and adopt the mid position, 'chudan-gamae'.

3 . Pivot to the left, transferring your weight to your left foot raise your sword into the 'hasso-gamae' position.

4 . Continue raising the sword and pivoting until you assume the upper or Jodan stance.

31

5 . Take a step forward with the right foot until your heels touch . . .

6 . . . then step forward again with the righ foot and begin a straight cut.

7 . Complete the cut so that the sword finishes at about knee height.

8 . Pivot to your left shifting your weight the left foot and raising the sword.

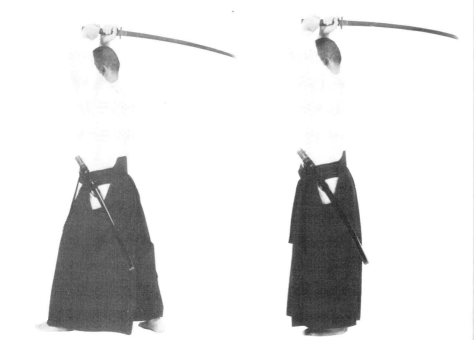

9 . Continue raising your sword until you are in the upper 'jodan' stance.

10 . Then stepping forward with the right foot until your heels touch . . .

11 . . . step forward with the right foot again, cutting as you do so . . .

12 . . . until the sword reaches the lower 'gedan' position. From this point, the exercise begins again from movement 1.

The Five Basic Drawing & Cutting Exercises

The purpose of these exercises is to develop a strong foundation upon which to build a superior sword method. As such it is obviously important that they are studied thoroughly and in depth, and the tendency to go on to more advanced and attractive techniques too quickly, avoided.

All the essential elements are included in these five basic movements. The rising cut, downward cut, side cut, one handed cut (nukiuchi) and thrust. They are combined into one step one cut movements which form the actual basis of the Toyama school sword drawing techniques, and upon which the more advanced double stepping methods of the Go Ho Batto Ho Jokyu exercises that follow in chapter 8, are based.

Another vital element that is learned from the five 'batto-ho' is the correct, and therefore the safe method of drawing and re-sheathing the sword. It cannot be stated too strongly that the incorrect draw and return of the sword to its scabbard, are very dangerous and can cause severe wounds to the hand if a real sword is being used for training. The batto-ho exercises should therefore be viewed as starting from the attention position and finishing in the same position, the drawing and re-sheathing of the sword are vital parts of the exercise, not simply actions that precede and follow the actual cutting techniques.

BREAKDOWN OF IMPORTANT POINTS OF EACH EXERCISE

Batto Ho No. 1
Teaches the side draw, left diagonal cut 'kesa-giri', mid-level stance 'chudan-kamae', removing blood from the sword at the end of the engagement 'jodan-chiburi', and re-sheathing the sword 'noto'.

Batto Ho No. 2
Right and left diagonal cuts, mid-level stance, cleaning the sword and re-sheathing it.

Batto Ho No. 3
Right rising cut 'kiri-age', left diagonal cut, mid-level stance, cleaning the sword and re-sheathing.

Batto Ho No. 4
Draw and one handed diagonal cut 'kesa-giri', but also called 'katate-kesa' or 'nuki-uchi', followed by a right diagonal cut, mid-level stance, cleaning and re-sheathing the sword.

Batto Ho No. 5
Drawing the sword close to the body, performing the thrust 'tsuki', followed by right diagonal cut, then cleaning and re-sheathing the sword.

Vocabulary for this section

KESA GIRI diagonal cut to the left or the right, from high to low level.
YOKO GIRI horizontal cut to the right or left.
KIRI AGE an upward diagonal cut from low to high level, right or left hand side.
TSUKI A straight thrust with the sword at an opponent's throat or chest.
JODAN upper level.
CHUDAN mid level.
GEDAN lower level.
KAMAE stance, i.e. 'chudan-kamae', mid-level stance.
CHIBURI cleaning the blade by flinging the blood from it.
NOTO re-sheathing the sword.

1. From the 'attention' position . . .

2 . . . step forward with the right foot, grasping the hilt of your sword as you do so.

5. As the cut is completed . . .

6 . . . bring your left foot up to your right, raising the sword into the upper or 'jodan' stance.

...

3 . Draw your sword and in one continuous motion . . .

4 . . . execute a horizontal cut to the side.

7 . Slide the left foot forward . . .

8 . . . and start to perform a diagonal cut . . .

9 . . . finishing the cut with the elbows against the body to prevent the sword hitting the floor.

10 . Maintaining full concentration, step forward with the right foot into the middle 'chudan' stance.

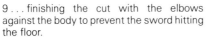
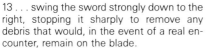

13 . . . swing the sword strongly down to the right, stopping it sharply to remove any debris that would, in the event of a real encounter, remain on the blade.

14 . Prepare to sheath your sword . . .

11. After a short pause, turn the blade outwards slightly and raise it to your right . . .

12 . . . then bringing your right hand in close to your forehead . . .

15 . . . then placing the point into the scabbard . . .

16 . . . push the blade home.

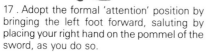

17 . Adopt the formal 'attention' position by bringing the left foot forward, saluting by placing your right hand on the pommel of the sword, as you do so.

18 . Finish the exercise by dropping your right hand to your side.

1. From the formal attention position . . .

2 . . . draw your sword as you step forward with the right foot . . .

3 . . . deflecting your opponent's attack as you continue to draw . . .

4 . . . to cut downwards along a diagonal line . . .

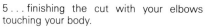

5 . . . finishing the cut with your elbows touching your body.

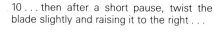

6 . Step forward with the left foot, raising your sword above your head as you do so . . .

9 . Maintaining your concentration, step forward with the right foot into the 'chudan-kamae' position . . .

10 . . . then after a short pause, twist the blade slightly and raising it to the right . . .

7 . . . then sliding the left foot forward, perform the diagonal 'kesa-giri' cut . . .

8 . . . completing it once again with the elbows against the body.

11 . . . bring the hilt close to your forehead . . .

12 . . . then swing the blade down to your right . . .

13 . . . stopping it abruptly in the position shown to remove anything soiling the blade.

14 . Prepare to sheath your sword.

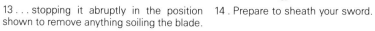

17 . Bring the left foot to the right, saluting with the hand on the pommel as you do so . . .

18 . . . and drop your right hand to your side to finish the exercise.

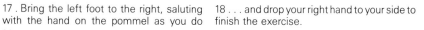

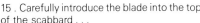

15 . Carefully introduce the blade into the top of the scabbard . . .

16 . . . and keeping your hand away from the edge, push it home.

1 . From the attention position . . .

2 . . . step forward with the right foot, unlocking your blade as you do so.

5 . Bring your left foot up to your right, raising your sword overhead as you do so . . .

6 . . . then sliding the left foot forward, perform a diagonal cut . . .

3 . Draw and cup upwards . . .

4 . . . at your opponent's ribs or forearms.

7 . . . finishing with the elbows touching the body.

8 . Maintaining your concentration, step forward with the right foot into the middle 'chudan' position.

9 . After a slight pause, twist the blade a little, and raising it to your right . . .

10 . . . take it close to your forehead . . .

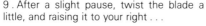

13 . Prepare to re-sheath your blade . . .

14 . . . and inserting the point into the scabbard . . .

11 . . . then snap it sharply down to the right . . .

12 . . . to remove any debris that may be soiling it.

15 . . . push it home.

16 . Bring the left foot upto the right, and salute by touching the end of the pommel . . .

17 . . . then drop the right hand to your side to
complete the exercise.

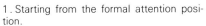

1. Starting from the formal attention position.

2. Step forward with the left foot as you take hold of your sword . . .

3 . . . and drawing it upwards until it clears the scabbard . . .

4 . . . make a single handed diagonal stroke 'kesa-giri' . . .

5 . . . to cut down an enemy standing on your right.

6 . Step forward with the right foot raising the hands into 'jodan-kamae' . . .

9 . Adopt the middle 'chudan' guard position . . .

10 . . . then after a short pause, twist the blade slightly and raising it to your right . . .

7 . . . then stepping forward again with the right foot, cut diagonally to your left . . .

8 . . . until the 'kesa-giri' technique is complete.

11 . . . take it around until your hand is close to your forehead . . .

12 . . . then swing it strongly downwards . . .

13 . . . stopping it abruptly to remove anything adhering to the blade.

14 . Prepare to sheath the sword by placing the back edge between the thumb and forefinger . . .

15 . . . then place the end of the blade into the scabbard, and push it home.

16 . Bring the left foot upto the right, saluting by touching the pommel as you do so.

17 . Drop the right hand to the side to finish
the exercise.

1. Starting in the attention position.

2. Grasp your sword and . . .

5. Thrust at your opponent's chest or throat . . .

6 . . . then withdrawing the blade from the target . . .

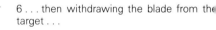

3 . . . sliding your right foot back, draw your blade . . .

4 . . . keeping it close to your body.

7 . . . raise it above your head . . .

8 . . . and take a step forward with the right foot until both feet are in line with, and touching each other.

9 . Step forward with the right foot and start to perform a left diagonal cut . . .

10 . . . finishing with the elbows touching the body to prevent loss of control of your blade.

13 . . . so your hand passes close to your forehead . . .

14 . . . perform chiburi, literally 'blood throwing off' . . .

1 . Maintaining your concentration adopt the middle guard position . . .

12 . . . then raising the sword and circling it around . . .

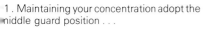

5 . . . snapping the blade to a halt to clean it.

16 . Prepare to re-sheath your blade . . .

17 . . . place it into the scabbard . . .

18 . . . and push it home.

19 . Bring your left foot upto your right, saluting by touching the pommel of the sword . . .

20 . . . and finish by dropping the right hand to the side.

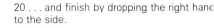

The Five Advanced Drawing & Cutting Exercises

The five advanced (jokyu) exercises follow on from the basic, and quite naturally are more complex and taxing to perform. They are designed to teach smooth continuous movement in which the feet, body and sword all function in unison.

Whereas in the five basic exercises the right foot was forward during the re-sheathing of the sword, in the advanced techniques the 'noto' is performed with the left foot forward, a more flexible position from which it is easier to deal with attacks from a variety of directions.

Practice should be very slow and deliberate at first so that bad habits are not picked up, and progress is steady. Later, speed will develop naturally, but it must never be forgotten that even if the actual cutting techniques can be performed very fast, drawing and re-sheathing the sword must be done with great care, even by a very expert swordsman. Self inflicted damage which results from careless drawing or re-sheathing, is often very serious.

Batto Ho Jokyu 1
A side draw and right diagonal cut performed in a single
movement, followed by a step backwards, sword cleaning and
re-sheathing.

Batto Ho Jokyu 2
The right 'kesa' to left 'kesa' is performed as one continuous
movement, the important thing to master is the body
movement that combines the two cutting techniques.

Batto Ho Jokyu 3
Perform the rising cut 'kiri-age', then turning the sword
edge, the downward diagonal cut, 'kesa-giri'. This should be
one continuous movement.

Batto Ho Jokyu 4
Draw the sword and perform 'nuki-uchi', then turning the
sword to the right of your body, follow with a right 'kesa-giri'.

Batto Ho Jokyu 5
Starts with a right 'kesa-giri', continues with a side cut and
concludes with a left 'kesa-giri' diagonal cut. Batto Ho Jokyu
1-4 teach two cutting techniques performed in one
continuous movement, while No. 5 teaches three.

. Starting in the formal attention posi-
on . . .

2 . . . step forward with the right foot as you take hold of your sword.

3 . Draw your sword . . .

4 . . . and perform a horizontal side cut.

5. Turn your wrist so the tip of the sword points to the rear . . .

6 . . . then bringing the left foot up to the right, circle the sword up and around . . .

9 . . . then cut diagonally downwards . . .

10 . . . finishing the cut with the elbows touching the body.

7 . . . and taking hold with your left hand . . .

8 . . . step forward with the left foot with the sword still raised above your head . . .

1. Move backwards slightly, turning your arm so that the palm faces downwards, then after a slight pause . . .

12 . . . start to re-sheath your sword.

13 . Place the sword into the scabbard as shown . . .

14 . . . and taking care to keep your hand away from the sharp edge . . .

15 . . . push it all the way home.

16 . Move the right foot up to the left . . .

17 . . . then salute by touching the pommel . . .   18 . . . and finish the exercise by dropping your right hand to your side.

1. From the attention position . . .

2 . . . draw your sword as you step forward with the right foot . . .

5 . . . in upper 'jodan' stance.

6 . Cut diagonally downward to your left . .

3 . . . circle it around to deflect the opponent's attack . . .

4 . . . and prepare to take hold of the sword with both hands . . .

7 . . . stopping the blade at the completion of the cut . . .

8 . . . then raising it to the side . . .

9 . . . bring it up into the 'hasso' position . . .

10 . . . then further up still until you assume 'jodan kamae', moving the left foot upto the right as you do so.

13 . . . 'kesa-giri'.

14 . Move backwards slightly, twisting your sword hand so the palm faces the floor . . .

11. Step forward with the left foot . . .

12 . . . and cut diagonally downwards to the right with . . .

15 . . . then after a slight pause, start to re-sheath the sword.

16. Insert the tip of the sword carefully into the scabbard as shown . . .

17 . . . and push it slowly and deliberately . . .   18 . . . all the way home.

19 . Bring your right foot upto the left so that   20 . . . and finish the exercise by dropping
the heels touch . . .   your right hand to your side.

1. From the formal attention position . . .

2 . . . step forward with the right foot and unlock the blade.

3. Start to draw the sword . . .

4 . . . and as it clears the scabbard . . .

5 . . . continue cutting upwards with your opponent's flank or forearms as the target.

6 . When the cut is completed . . .

9 . . . and taking a left step forward . . .

10 . . . cut diagonally to your left . . .

7 . . . twist your sword hand so that the palm faces to the left . . .

8 . . . then moving the left foot upto the right, take hold of the sword with both hands . . .

11 . . . finishing the cut with the elbows touching the body.

12 . Move backwards slightly twisting the sword hand so the palm faces the ground . . .

13 . . . then after a slight pause, start to re-sheath the sword.

14 . Insert the sword into the scabbard . . .

17 . Move the left foot upto the right until the heels are together . . .

18 . . . then touching the pommel in salute . . .

15 . . . then push it slowly and smoothly . . .   16 . . . all the way home.

19 . . . drop your right hand to your side to finish the exercise.

1. From the basic standing position . . .

2 . . . step forward with the left foot, taking hold of the sword as you do so.

5 . . . as if to cut down an opponent in front of you.

6 . Turn the sword so the tip points to the rear . . .

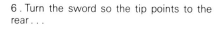

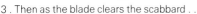

3 . Then as the blade clears the scabbard . . .   4 . . . cut strongly downwards and to your right with the right hand . . .

7 . . . then raising the sword above your head . . .   8 . . . take hold of it with both hands in 'jodan-kamae' stance.

9 . Step forward with the right foot and cut diagonally to your left . . .

10 . . . on the completion of the cut . . .

13 . . . step back with the right foot and move the sword out to the right so the tip is at knee level.

14 . Start to re-sheath the sword.

11 . . . take the right foot back to the left . . .

12 . . . and taking hold of the scabbard with the left hand, turn the sword so that it faces slightly to the right . . .

15 . Insert the tip into the mouth of the scabbard . . .

16 . . . and slowly and calmly . . .

17 . . . push it all the way home.

18 . Bring the right foot upto the left, saluting as you do so by touching the pommel.

19 . Drop your right hand from the sword to your side, to finish the exercise.

1. From the basic starting position . . .   2 . . . take hold of the sword . . .

3 . . . and step back with the right foot as you   4 . . . continuing the movement with a hori-
draw to the side . . .   zontal cut . . .

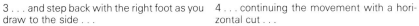

5 . . . then raising the sword up and around . . .

6 . . . bring the right foot up to the left, raising the sword overhead as you do so.

9 . . . finishing with the elbows touching the body to prevent the sword touching the ground.

10 . Twist the hands so the edge faces to the left . . .

7 . Step forward with the right foot . . .

8 . . . and perform a diagonal cut . . .

11 . . . then stepping back with the right foot until both feet are touching . . .

12 . . . step to the right with the right foot, starting a right horizontal cut as you do so.

13 . As you complete the cut . . .

14 . . . . turn the sword to face the rear, edge up . . .

17 . . . and cut diagonally downwards with 'kesa-giri'.

18 . On the completion of the cut . . .

15 . . . then bringing the left foot up to the right, raise the sword overhead.

16 . Step forward with the left foot . . .

19 . . . move backwards slightly, turning the sword hand so that the palm faces the floor . . .

20 . . . then after a slight pause, start to re-sheath the sword . . .

21 . . . insert the point into the mouth of the scabbard . . .

22 . . . and slowly and deliberately . . .

25 . . . and saluting by touching the pommel of the sword . . .

26 . . . drop the right hand to the side to finish the exercise.

23 . . . push it all the way home.

24 . Bring the right foot upto the left . . .

9

Shodan No Kata

初段の型

This exercise teaches the practical applications of the Toyama Ryu eight cuts exercise (happo giri — see 'Naked Blade' by the same author) against an enemy in front of you. It is good training for real test cutting, which in the normal course of events would be taught when this kata was mastered. Serious study of Shodan no Kata, will also instil in the student the understanding of varying speed of physical movement, eg. fast-slow-fast when performing cuts, and also help him develop the calmness of mind and spirit so necessary for the practical swordsman.

1. From the formal standing position . . .

2 . . . drop into a squatting position 'sonkyo' by sitting on the heels . . .

3 . . . then stand upright, taking hold of the sword, and easing the blade out slightly by pushing against the guard with the left thumb.

4 . Move the right foot to the right as you draw the sword . . .

5 . . . and continue drawing until the sword clears the scabbard.

6 . Drop the sword to the side on the completion of the draw . . .

9 . . . and continue to raise it until you assume the upper 'jodan' stance.

10 . Move the left foot back to the right . . .

7 . . . and move the left foot upto the right until they touch.

8 . As you take a step forward with the left foot, raise the sword on the centre line of the body . . .

11 . . . then move the left foot out to the left as you begin a diagonal 'kesa-giri' cut.

12 . On the completion of the cut . . .

93

13 . . . move the right foot upto the left . . .

14 . . . and twist the hands so the point of the sword is carried towards the rear . . .

17 . On the completion of the cut, twist the hands so the sword points to the rear . . .

18 . . . then drawing the right foot back to the left . . .

15 . . . then stepping forward with the right foot, start to perform . . .

16 . . . a horizontal cut to the right.

19 . . . step to the right with the right foot . . .

20 . . . and perform a diagonal cut to the right.

21. As the cut is completed . . .

22 . . . turn the sword so the edge is facing forward . . .

25 . . . take the sword around to your left . . .

26 . . . and prepare to attack by pointing the right foot forwards . . .

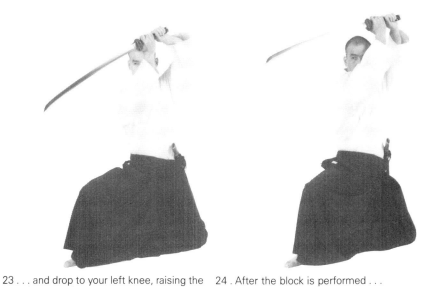

23 . . . and drop to your left knee, raising the sword as you do so.

24 . After the block is performed . . .

27 . . . then start to perform a rising cut, 'kiri-age' . . .

28 . . . finishing in the position shown.

29 . Drop the sword to the side of your body, close in and with the point to the front . . .

30 . . . and standing, while maintaining the same position . . .

33 . . . and raise it overhead as shown.

34 . Bring the left foot back to the right and assume 'jodan' stance . . .

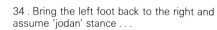

31 . . . take a left step forward and thrust your sword into the enemy.

32 . Withdraw the blade from the target . . .

35 . . . then moving the left foot out to the side . . .

36 . . . cut straight down along the centre line of the body . . .

37 . . . until the technique is completed and the elbows are touching the body.

38 . Move the left foot up to the right . . .

41 . . . around to the right . . .

42 . . . until the sword hand is close to the forehead . . .

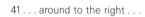

39 . . . then with the sword held in the middle or 'chudan' position, step back with the left foot.

40 . Take hold of the scabbard with the left hand, as you raise the sword . . .

43 . . . and perform 'chiburi' by swinging the blade down to your right . . .

44 . . . stopping it abruptly to remove anything that may be adhering to the blade.

45 . Move the left foot up to the right . . .

46 . . . then stepping backwards with the right foot . . .

49 . . . and taking care at all times to keep your left hand clear of the sword edge . . .

50 . . . push the blade home.

47 . . . prepare to re-sheath your sword.

48 . Raise the hilt so the point enters the mouth of the scabbard . . .

51 . Salute by touching the pommel of the sword . . .

52 . . . then adopt the closing position by dropping the right hand to the side.

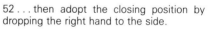

10

Nidan No Kata

This exercise is more practical than the one that precedes it and teaches how to defend against and reply to assaults from enemies to the front and rear.

貳段の型

1. From the attention position . . .

2 . . . step forward with the right foot and unlock the blade . . .

3 . . . draw the sword and assume the middle 'chudan' stance.

4 . Raise the sword into the upper 'jodan' position . . .

5 . . . and step forward with the left foot . . . 6 . . . then the right . . .

9 . Raise the sword back into the middle position . . . 10 . . . then up into 'jodan-kamae' . . .

7 . . . and cut straight down along the centre line of the body.

8 . Movements 4~8 are performed as one rapid jumping cutting sequence finishing at this point.

11 . . . and bringing the left foot upto the right . . .

12 . . . step forward with the left foot again cutting diagonally downwards . . .

13 . . . until the 'kesa-giri' technique is completed.

14 . Twisting the hands to carry the point of the sword to the rear . . .

17 . Step back with the left foot . . .

18 . . . and back again cutting diagonally downwards as you do so . . .

15 . . . raise it to the side until . . .

16 . . . you assume the 'jodan-kamae' position.

19 . . . until the technique is completed.

20 . Step forward with the left foot . . .

21 . . . then pivot clockwise on the left foot . . .   Side View.

23 . . . to the rear.   Side View.

22 . . . performing a horizontal cut . . .   Side View.

24 . Step forward with the right foot, and pull   Side View.
the sword back and in to your right side as
you do so . . .

25 . . . and thrust at your opponent.   Side View.

27 . . . and thrust again.   Side View.

26 . Step forward with the left foot, and pull back your sword to your side . . .

Side View.

28 . Jump back two steps as you block your opponent's counter attack with your raised sword . . .

Side View.

29 . . . then assuming the 'jodan' position, move the left foot upto the right.   Side View.

31 . . . finishing in the position shown.   Side View.

30 . Move your left foot out as you perform 'kesa-giri' . . .

Side View.

32 . Turn the sword to the left so that the point is towards the rear . . .

Side View.

33 . . . then moving the right foot up to the left . . .

34 . Step forward with the right foot and perform a horizontal cut to the side.

Side View.

36 . . . step forward with the left foot . . .

Side View.

35 . As the cut is completed . . .

37 . . . then raising the sword and pivoting around . . .

38 . . . assume the 'jodan' position.

39 . At the instant the turn is completed . . .

40 . . . cut straight down along the centre line of the body.

43 . Assume the 'jodan' position . . .

44 . . . then stepping forward with the right foot, perform the diagonal 'kesa-giri' cut . . .

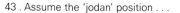

41. Step forward with the left foot, raising your sword . . .

42 . . . to deflect an attack in the movement called 'suriage'.

45 . . . stopping the blade at the position shown.

46 . Draw the blade back . . .

47 . . . then step back with the right foot as you continue to raise the blade . . .

48 . . . to block your opponent's attack.

51 . Step to the left and perform a downwards diagonal 'kesa-giri' cut.

52 . As the cut is completed . . .

9 . Step back with the left foot as you bring your sword around in an anti-clockwise direction . . .

50 . . . until you assume the upper or 'jodan' guard position.

3 . . . move the right foot up to the left, holding the sword as shown . . .

54 . . . and circle the blade up into the 'jodan' position . . .

55 . . . then moving the left foot out to the left . . .

56 . . . perform 'kesa-giri' . . .

59 . . . then step back with the left to adopt the middle or 'chudan' position.

60 . Clean the blade by flicking it to the right . . .

7 . . . finishing in the position shown.

58 . Bring the left foot upto the right . . .

1 . . . and prepare to re-sheath the sword y . . .

62 . . . inserting the point into the mouth of the scabbard . . .

63 . . . and pushing it carefully . . .

64 . . . all the way home.

65 . Perform the formal salute by touching the end of the pommel . . .

66 . . . and drop the right hand to the side t finish the exercise.

11

The practice of test cutting, 'tameshigiri' or 'shizan',
distinguishes practical styles of swordsmanship
(Toyama, and Ioriken schools) from the philosophical and
sporting (iaido and kendo). It is an essential discipline for
those who wish to become true swordsmen, for only by
cutting realistic targets can the three essential elements of
swordsmanship; grip, edge placement and control of the
blade be learnt and understood.

The grip, 'tenouchi' must be correctly formed and strong.
The angle that the sharp edge of the sword engages the
target, 'hasuji' must be precise otherwise the blade may
break, or the wrists be damaged. The blade must be stopped
correctly 'tome', or the swordsman may suffer severe injury
from his own weapon. Swordsmanship without test cutting is
as useful as marksmanship without bullets. Only by cutting
can ability be evaluated, there is no exception to this rule.
Schools that maintain that tameshigiri is not necessary,
cannot be regarded as effective methods of swordsmanship.

Initially the student should practice left and right 'kesa' cuts
on targets such as wet straw bundles or bamboo, then
progress to side cuts right and left so as to learn correct body
shifting which is an essential element in 'yoko-giri'. Finally
the left and right upward cuts, 'kiri-age' should be attempted
as they are the most difficult in the Toyama Ryu repertoire
to master. They are in fact so difficult to master that even
during the Edo period (1600-1868), swordsmen that were
proficient in 'kiri-age' were rare. Then as now, kesa-giri was
the most common cut used in actual combat.

試し斬り

One of the most famous exponents of the difficult upward cut was Yagyu Munenori, one of the renowned line of Yagyu School swordsmen that served the Tokugawa Shoguns for almost three centuries. At the battle of Osaka Castle in 1616 (Natsu no Jin) he was the military strategist to Tokugawa Ieyasu, as well as his personal bodyguard.

The furious onslaught of the enemy Samurai during one of the bitterest phases of the campaign, broke the ranks of close retainers around Ieyasu (Hatamoto) and left him vulnerable, save for his trusted retainer. On that bloody day, Yagyu Munenori killed eight armoured samurai by striking up at them from below with 'kiri-age', a tremendous feat that could only have been performed by a master swordsman. This technique was especially effective on the battlefield because Samurai armour was designed to defeat attacks from above such as straight or diagonal downward cuts. As a result of this, and to save weight and maximise the wearer's mobility, the under surfaces of the armour were only lightly protected, and therefore vulnerable to 'kiri-age'.

From that time forth, the Yagyu family served the Tokugawa Shoguns as sword masters and advisers, and enjoyed their complete trust and confidence. Munenori taught swordsmanship to the second Shogun Hidetada, and later to the third Iemitsu, to whom he was also a senior adviser, 'so-metsuke'. At the height of his career he received a stipend of 12,500 Koku (one koku is about four and a half bushels, or enough rice to feed one man for one year), and had the status equivalent to that of a provincial lord.

After you have mastered the single cutting strokes, it is time to move on to double and triple cutting of targets. For example, 'kesa-giri' and 'kiri-age' or 'kesa-giri' and 'yoko-giri' both performed as one movement. After all, on the battlefield you cannot stop after each cut to see if you have killed your opponent or not, you simply keep fighting.

HIDARI KESA GIRI

The left and right diagonal cuts (kesa-giri) are the most basic, powerful and useful techniques, and therefore the most often used in combat. Right kesa-giri (not illustrated) is a natural movement that with practice is relatively easy to learn. Left kesa-giri while less powerful, will often cut more cleanly because the grip automatically tightens as the technique is performed, and this improves the cutting action.

SHIN CHOKU GIRI (STRAIGHT CUT)

This technique was frequently used for sword testing and depends for flawless performance on correct grip and perfect balance of power between the arms. In the old days, when it was known as 'suemono-giri' it was used to test swords on the bodies of executed criminals which were laid on top of each other. The record number of bodies cut in two with one cut is seven.

HIDARI MAYOKO-GIRI (LEFT SIDE CUT)

A very difficult technique to master, but useful on the battlefield when fighting several opponents at the same time.

MIGI MAYOKO-GIRI (RIGHT SIDE CUT)

This technique is often performed as 'nuki-uchi', simultaneous drawing and cutting. It is useful in a combat situation for removing an enemy's head.

MIGI KIRIAGE (RIGHT RISING CUT)

A very advanced technique that is difficult to master. Useful when performing 'nuki-uchi', draw and simultaneous cut or 'tsubame-gaeshi'. (Literally swallow cut, a right diagonal cut followed without hesitation by a right rising cut.)

HIDARI KIRIAGE (LEFT RISING CUT)

Both right and left rising cuts are very difficult to master, and therefore rarely seen these days. They require perfect balance and application of power if the cut is to be cleanly made.

12

Sword Care

日本刀鑑賞

A complete etiquette grew around the use and handling of the sword during the time that Samurai were masters of Japan, but it was one that was practical and founded upon basic common sense and good manners. If you wish to become a swordsman, you must first understand the etiquette of handling the sword.

For example, it has always been considered unwise to pick up another man's sword without his permission, you could pay for such an insult with your life. You did not withdraw another man's blade to view it, other than in slow easy movements that would not alarm your host or give him cause to defend himself, and only then with his permission. Nor did you touch a blade, because the sweat your fingers left on its surface could ruin the beauty imparted by the sword polisher's dedicated and time consuming work. Similarly, you did not breathe upon the surface of the steel for fear of leaving a film of moisture that would turn it to rust.

These are things the modern swordsman must understand, for they are as valid today as they were in feudal times. They teach respect for the possessions of others, self control and mental discipline which are major weapons in the martial artist's greatest battle, against that principal enemy of all that seek perfection, ego!

1. Sit in the formal 'seiza' position with your sword and cleaning materials close at hand. Relax and calm your mind.

2. Take the sword in your left hand . . .

5 . . . and place the scabbard carefully on the floor to your left . . .

6 . . . ready for when you will need it again.

3 . . . and raising it before you, show your respect for it by bowing slightly.

4 . Unsheath the blade in one movement, quietly and smoothly . . .

7 . Taking the sword in both hands, carefully inspect it for obvious damage . . .

8 . . . then taking a very soft cleaning cloth folded into a thick wad . . .

9 . . . check all the 'working' areas for chips, cracks or other defects . . .

10 . . . especially the part of the blade used for cutting, the 'monouchi' from the tip to about one third the way along the blade.

13 . Remove the blade carefully from the hilt . . .

14 . . . then the guard and washers that fit on either side of it . . .

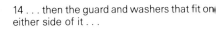

11. Using a special little hammer 'mekugi-nuki', drive the retaining peg out of the handle . . .

12 . . . holding the hilt 'tsukagashira', strike your left hand, smartly with your right to loosen the sword from the handle.

15 . . . then finally the blade collar or 'habaki' that locates the blade in the scabbard.

16 . Now the blade is ready for your attention, so pause for a moment to enjoy it before proceeding.

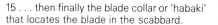

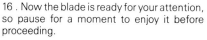

17 . Using special cleaning paper, or if you don't have any, clean soft face tissue, remove any old oil from the blade.

18 . Apply special sword powder 'uchiko' to both sides of the blade . . .

21 . . . clean the blade, using slow even strokes away from you.

22 . Examine the whole sword again . . .

19 . . . evenly, using the small applicator.

20 . Then using more clean sword paper or tissue . . .

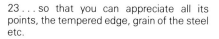

23 . . . so that you can appreciate all its points, the tempered edge, grain of the steel etc.

24 . Lightly oil the blade with sword oil, do not overdo this otherwise you will soil the inside of the scabbard and ruin it. In very dry countries, the application of oil to prevent rusting is hardly necessary.

25 . Re-install the blade collar, 'habaki' . . .

26 . . . followed by the hand guard with a metal washer 'seppa' on either side.

29 . Push the peg 'mekugi' into the hole . . .

30 . . . and tap it lightly with the little hammer to ensure a firm fit.

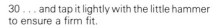

27 . Refit the handle to the blade . . .

28 . . . then holding it in the left hand, tap it with your right until the holes in the handle and the blade are in line.

31 . Check to make sure nothing is loose and that the handle and the blade are properly mated together . . .

32 . . . make a final check that the blade is in good order . . .

33 . . . then take up the scabbard . . .

34 . . . and inserting the blade into it taking care to see that only the back edge of the sword is in contact with the inside of the scabbard . . .

37 . . . and lowering it to your side . . .

38 . . . finally place it on the floor to your left to finish your sword maintenance routine.

35 . . . with a single movement, quietly and smoothly push the blade home.

36 . Bow to the sword . . .

Glossary

Batto-jutsu   The art of drawing and simultaneously cutting with the sword.

Chudan-kamae   The middle stance with the sword in which it is held straight in front of the body with the point directed towards the throat of the adversary.

Gedan-kamae   The lower stance in which the sword is held in front of the body with the end pointing downwards.

Habaki   A metal collar that fits on the sword blade where it enters the handle and serves to locate it in the scabbard.

Ichimonji-Suburi   Practice or empty cutting to improve the co-ordination between body and sword.

Jodan-kamae   The upper stance in which the sword is held above the head with both hands.

Jokyu   Advanced techniques as in Batto Ho Jokyu advanced sword drawing method.

Kata   A formal exercise of unvarying movements.

Kesa Giri   A diagonal downward cut with the sword, named after a type of sash or bib worn by some Buddhist priests which when in position over the shoulder and across the body, exactly describes the path taken by the sword when this cut is made.

Kiri-age   A very difficult cut, usually used only by master swordsmen, in which the sword travels upwards and diagonally. (see page 132).

Mekugi   The small wooden peg that secures the blade in the handle of the sword.

Mekugi-ana   The hole in the sword tang that accommodates the 'mekugi'.

Mekugi-nuki   Small brass mallet or hammer used to remove or fit the sword peg 'mekugi' to the sword.

Nidan   Second or number two.

Seppa   Washers that are fitted to either side of the sword guard.

Shodan   First or number one.

Sonkyo   A squatting position.

Tameshigiri   Test cutting on special targets, bamboo straw bundles etc.

Tsuba   The sword guard.

Tsukagashira   The hilt of the sword.

Tsuki   A thrust with the sword.

Yoko-giri   A cut to the side.

Bibliography

NIPPON TO MONOGATARI
by Fukunaga Suiken published by Yuzankaku.

KUBIKIRI ASAEMON TO KEN OSHIGATA
by Fukunaga Suiken.

ZIDAI KOSHO ZITEN
by Inagaki Shisei published by Shinjinbutsu Oraisha.

NIHON BUDO ZITEN
by Kasama Yoshihiko published by Kashiwa Shobo.

KIREAJI NIPPON TO
published by Kogei Shuppan.

TATAKAU NIPPON TO
by Naruse Kanji.

MEIJI KABUTOWARI
by Tsumoto Yo published by Kodansha.

NIPPON TO TAMESHIGIRI NO SHINZUI
by Nakamura Taizaburo published by Kodansha.

MEITO TO MEISHO
by Fukunaga Suiken published by Yuzankaku.

BUSHO TO SONO AITO
by Sato Kanzan published by Shinjinbutsu Oraisha.

JIDAI KOSHO HYAKKA
by Nawa Yumio published by Shinjinbutsu Oraisha.

Author's names appear in the Japanese manner, that is
Family name first and given name second.

Nunchaku Dynamic Training
BY HIROKAZU KANAZAWA 8TH DAN
Former three time All Japan Karate Champion, and supreme master of the Shotokan style of karate, the author is also a recognised weapons expert, specialising in nunchaku and sai. His book has been acclaimed as the best produced, and easiest to understand on the subject, and takes the reader right from the most basic movements, up to a complex and dynamic 106 move kata, that develops technique and style, as well as providing a dazzling exhibition of skill for demonstration purposes. An in depth work that includes sections on history, origins, author's biography, health aspects etc. 160 pages (9" x 6") laminated full colour cover. **$9.95**

Shotokan Advanced Kata Series
BY KEINOSUKE ENOEDA 8TH DAN
Nicknamed the "Shotokan Tiger" by the students and instructors of the prestigious JKA Instructors Institute, this explosive and powerful teacher, who is noted for his practical fighting ability, must surely be the best possible person to present this important series of books. A perfectionist in all he does, the author shows by means of individually hand printed and prepared photographs, and detailed captions, every single movement of these intricate exercises with a degree of clarity never before achieved. A series that should find its way into the collection of every martial artist.

Vol 1 Bassai Dai:Kanku Dai:Jion:Empi:Hangetsu
8" x 12" 140 pages **$14.95**
Vol 2 Bassai Sho:Bassai Dai:Jiin:Gankaku:Sochin
8" x 12" 111 pages **$14.95**
Vol 3 Tekki-Nidan:Tekki-Sandan (2 versions):Nijushiho:
Gojushiho-Dai:Gojushiho-Sho
8" x 12" 111 pages **£14.95**

Shadow of the Ninja
BY KATSUMI TODA
The extensive martial arts and historical knowledge of the author, gives an authenticity and depth to this stirring tale of the Samurai Kuroda and the Ninja of the Tomokatsu clan, that will hold the reader spellbound throughout this beautifully produced book. A fast moving tale of treachery, sudden death and martial excellence in 17th century Japan, made all the more fascinating by original illustrations of Ninja weaponry and techniques. Nine sell-out editions in 25 months proves our claim that "Shadow of the Ninja" sets a new standard for books of this type in quality of production, design and content. 8" x 5" 127 pages **$7.95**

Revenge of the Shogun's Ninja
BY KATSUMI TODA
In this sequel to the best selling novel "Shadow of the Ninja" the feud between the Tomokatsu Ninja Clan and the Kuroda Samurai family, moves on a generation as it approaches its dramatic and bloodthirsty conclusion. The secrets of the Ninja are pitted against the supernatural powers of the masters of the spirit of the wind, as the Tomokatsu clan seek out the ghostly green warriors of the forests of Kyushu, for a final dramatic confrontation. An action packed story, full of accurate and intriguing information and lavishly illustrated with line drawings of Ninja techniques and equipment. 8" x 5" 107 pages **$7.95**

Ninja Death Vow
BY KATSUMI TODA
As sales of "Shadow of the Ninja" and "Revenge of the Shogun's Ninja" continue to soar, martial arts historian Katsumi Toda, presents the third part of the saga of the Tomokatsu Ninja and their enemies, the Kuroda Samurai. Set against the background of the U.S. Navy's incursion into Japanese waters just over a century ago to break down the barriers of isolation that had existed since 1600, it is a fast moving tale of revenge and treachery. When the Americans threaten to return at a later date and complete their mission, forces who wish to maintain the old system, let loose the power of Ninjutsu to aid their cause, and death and destruction stalk the land. Toda's fast moving style make the reader feel part of the story; just a page or two into the first chapter, and one can imagine standing on the deck of Commodore Mathew Perry's ship "Mississippi" as the Stars and Stripes fly for the first time over the Japanese waters of Uraga Bay. 144 pages 8½" x 5½" **$7.95**

The Ninja Star – Art of Shurikenjutsu
BY KATSUMI TODA
Noted Japanese martial arts historian, Katsumi Toda, reveals for the first time the results of his research into the art of star and spike throwing, as practised by the Ninja of medieval Japan. A complete work on this fascinating subject, the book includes; historical background, the development of Ninjutsu, types of shuriken and shaken, stances and grips, throwing techniques, targets, breathing exercises, kata and much more. Lavishly illustrated with attractive line drawings, it is a factual historical work, as well as a practical, down to earth "how to do it" book, and will therefore appeal to martial arts enthusiasts of all ages, styles and affiliations. 79 pages 9" x 6" full colour laminated cover, more than 110 illustrations. **$6.95**

Kubotan Keychain – Instrument of Attitude Adjustment
BY TAKAYUKI KUBOTA 8TH DAN
Known to millions as a result of his frequent screen and television apprearances, Takayuki Kubota, is a karate master and law-enforcement instructor of exeptional ability, who for two decades has coached the LAPD and other agencies at the highest level. His invention of the "Kubotan" a small plastic baton, (later converted to a keychain) for use by female police officers, revolutionised self-defence in the 70's, and the "Kubotan" itself has become recognised with the passage of time, as probably the most effective, legal self defense aid available to the citizen. In this detailed manual, its inventor shows a wide variety of methods for using the "Kubotan" in almost every imaginable situation. Detailed, high definition photographs and easy to understand text, allow the reader to quickly and fully understand the fine detail of how, and to what parts of the body, the Kubotan can be applied, in order to subdue even the unruliest agressor. Complete with striking points diagrams, grappling and striking techniques as well as a large selection of the very latest "Kubotan" techniques, the book represents the 'state of the art' in this field. Includes an introduction by Hollywood actor James Caan, 9" x 6" 104 pages full colour laminated cover **$7.95**

Dynamic Kicking Method
BY MASAFUMI SHIOMITSU 7TH DAN
There have been so many books on the subject of Karate's kicking techniques, that it is difficult to imagine one that would stand out against the background of boring and often repetitive books currently available. Due to a combination of author ability, excellent design and high quality photography, this one not only stands out, it shines! Author Shiomitsu is an absolute master of the karate kick, not just a talented dilettante, the techniques that he demonstrates and teaches are the original techniques of karate, before they were diluted and packaged for the western market place and are therefore, uncompromisingly tough and brutally effective, rather than athletic or as has been happening of late, theatrical. In this detailed text he not only teaches and demonstrates these techniques, but also includes information on how training and teaching techniques have changed as a result of the efforts to 'sanitize' karate in order to make it an acceptable sport, rather than an effective means of self defence, as well as stories of karate masters who made one or other of these deadly techniques their speciality. Within the covers of this book, is a wealth of information that it would take a lifetime of training to discover. Kicks to cause discomfort, pain, serious injury or worse, depending on the circumstances, and the way that they must be practised to be perfected. These techniques, and his performance of them, have earned the author an awesome reputation, as a particularly hard and dangerous fighter. This encyclopedic work can only endorse the reputation he has acquired as a result of his many victories in and out of the arena over the years. 9″ x 6″ 132 pages colour cover **$9.95**

Balisong – Iron Butterfly
BY CACOY "BOY" HERNANDEZ
We must warn the reader that this is not an instructional book in the normal sense of the word. The techniques showing the Balisong expert Cacoy Hernandez, were developed for, and can only be used in violent circumstances; they have no spiritual value whatsoever. Cacoy ("Boy" to his few friends), Hernandez, is a fighter of the old school, rather than one of the 'actors' that currently seem to dominate the martial arts scene. Born into poverty, raised in deprivation and matured against a background of criminality, he was forced to adopt survival methods, which, although shunned by modern urban society, have allowed him to enjoy six decades, and walk away from countless confrontations. Signor Hernandez has one unshakable belief, which can be summed up by the phrase "Never reject a challenge, and never step back." This book combining as it does his Balisong technique, together with accounts of incidents in his life when he has been forced to use it, must without doubt be of interest to all martial artists. 9″ x 6″ full colour cover, 107 pages **$7.95**

Naked Blade – A Manual of Samurai Swordmanship
BY TOSHISHIRO OBATA 7TH DAN
Long hidden from the gaze of all but the chosen few the ferocious techniques of swordsmanship as taught by the "Rikugun Toyama Gakko" are revealed for the first time in the English language in this comprehensive and well produced book. Author Toshishiro Obata, is an imposing and highly skilled exponent of this sword method of the former Japanese Imperial Army. The art that he demonstrates, was so feared in the West during the last global conflict that a military training manual published at the time was prompted to advise American officers to "Shoot the officers [with swords] first" as a matter of urgency when confronting the enemy for the first time. The strength, resolve and power of the Samurai lives through the techniques that they developed; they can find no finer repository than in the skill of the author and between the pages of this fascinating training manual. 6″ x 9″ 132 pages **$9.95**

Ninja Training Manual – A Treasury of Techniques
BY YUKISHIRO SANADA
Through an unbroken chain of many generations of Ninja Warriors that stretches back through the centuries of warfare, violence and treachery to the very roots of Japanese history come the original and authentic secrets of the Ninjutsu, many being presented here in written form for the first time. **$9.95**

Ninja Sword – Art of Silent Kenjutsu
BY KATSUMI TODA
Besides being expert with weapons like the Kama, Shuriken, Kaginawa and Manrikigusari for which they are best known, the Ninja trained hard to make themselves invincible with the beautiful but deadly Japanese sword. Ninja Sword – Art of Silent Kenjutsu contains much material only previously available to martial arts historians, and very senior exponents of the ancient art of Ninjutsu. As such it offers the reader a fascinating glimpse of the "Kage No Gundan" Japan's army of Shadow Warriors, their methods and their way of life. **$7.95**

Dynamic Power of Karate
BY HIROKAZO KANAZAWA 8TH DAN
Dynamic Power welded to awesome technical ability have made Karate's 'Iron Man', Hirokazu Kanazawa a legend in his own lifetime and an inspiration to his tens of thousands of students worldwide. A three time All Japan Karate champion and one of Karate's original and most active pioneers of the sixties and seventies, he has for the past twenty years set his peers and those that have followed, a standard of excellence that was always virtually impossible to equal and that remains to this day, impossible to exceed. **$14.95**

Kama – Weapon Art of Okinawa
BY TOSHISHORO OBATA
From the time that the warlord Hideyoshi outlawed the
ownership of edged weapons by Okinawans, the techniques
demonstrated in this book were kept hidden from the civil
and military authorities, and taught only in complete secrecy
to family members or "inner" students. Shogun Hideyoshi
had good reason to respect the fighting ability of the
islanders, for as author Toshishiro Obata shows, the twin
sickles of Okinawa are among the most effective close combat weapons ever invented, and when wielded by an expert,
almost unbeatable. 160 pages, 9˝ x 6˝ full colour laminated
cover. **$9.95**

When The Going Gets Tough
BY COLONEL M. SMYTHE
Not for the faint hearted or those of a nervous disposition,
the author's unique system of self-defence is simple but
appallingly effective. Developed from personal experience
during his active service career, it is to the urban misfit what
penicillin is to the germ. 9˝ x 6˝ full colour laminated cover.
$7.95

Forthcoming Titles

The Japanese Sword – A guide for Swordsmen and Collectors by T. Obata
Heiho Okugi Sho – The Inner Secrets of Martial Strategy by Kansuke Yamamoto
Samurai Aikijujutsu by T. Obata
Ninja – The Men of Iga by Shinichi Kano
Shotokan Advanced Kata Vol 4. by Keinosuke Enoeda.

Dragon Books are available from branches of B. Dalton Booksellers, Walden Books and all good martial arts
and general bookstores. If you have difficulty obtaining any of these titles, please contact the publisher direct.
Orders under $10 can be filled for the advertised price plus $1.50. For orders over $10 simply add 10% to the value
of your order to cover freight and handling charges. Overseas customers, please contact us for details of export
shipping costs. U.K. Distributor: Sakura Publications P.O. Box 18, Ashtead Surrey KT21 2JD.

Dragon Books P.O. Box 6039 Thousand Oaks CA 91359 USA

Phototypeset in the United Kingdom by Concise Graphics Ltd. Hammersmith London